IN THE BEGINNING

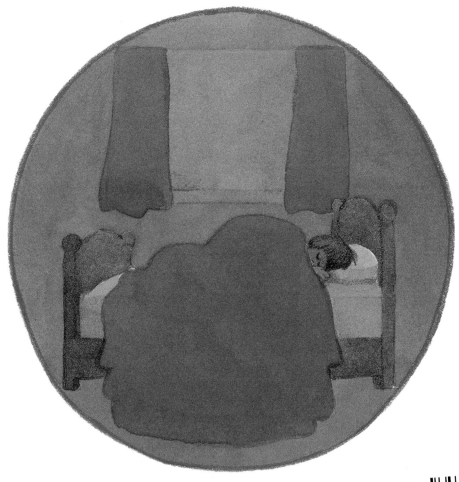

Miriam Ramsfelder Levin

illustrated by

Katherine Janus Kahn

KAR-BEN COPIES, INC.   ROCKVILLE, MD

To my three children:
Eric, who through his love of books has inspired me to write,
Jeremy, whose strength of character has taught me to persevere, and
Rebecca, whose birth has shown me that all things are possible.
—MRL

To Robert, the star of all my creations.
—KJK

Library of Congress Cataloging-in-Publication Data

Levin, Miriam
    In the beginning / Miriam Levin : illustrated by Katherine Janus Kahn.
      p. cm.
    Summary: In this adaptation of the creation story, Adam awakes, surveys his room and the larger world, decides that all is good, and then proceeds to deal with his loneliness.
    ISBN 0-929371-94-1. — ISBN 0-929371-95-X (pbk.)
    [1. Creation—Fiction.] I. Kahn, Katherine, ill. II. Title.
    [E] —dc20

                                 96-4172
                                   CIP
                                   AC

Published by KAR-BEN COPIES, INC. Rockville, MD 1-800-4KARBEN
Printed in the United States of America

IN THE BEGINNING

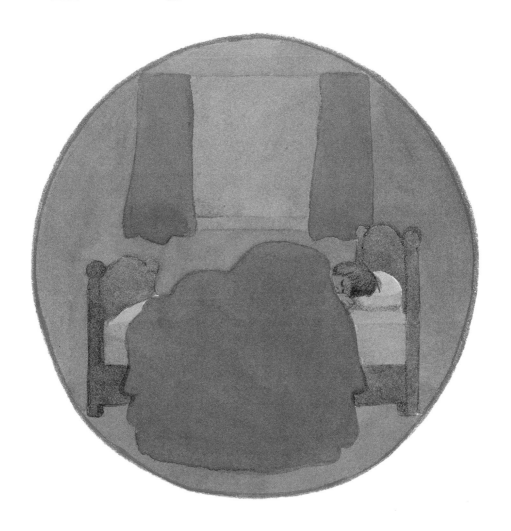

*The Talmud says that we have been
chosen by God
as partners in creation.*

Adam woke up.
It was dark and cold outside.
He was alone.

He turned on the light in his room.
What a mess, he thought, as he looked
around. His toys were scattered
everywhere. His matchbox cars were
mixed in with his Chinese checkers,
and paper and crayons littered the floor.

Building blocks were dumped into a
mountainous pile waiting to be formed
into a skyscraper, or a highway, or a
bridge. Adam looked at his room in the
light, and even though it was messy, he
saw that it was good.

Adam whirled around

pretending he was the wind.

The breeze carried his toys into the air.

Soon his room was neat, and he was glad.

Adam peeked at the windowsill garden
he had started at school. Tiny pea plants
had broken through the dark, damp soil.
The earth felt cool and soft.

He put his nose to the plant and took
a deep breath. It smelled like his
backyard right after the rain. Adam
had learned that plants and trees give
us food and oxygen, and he knew that
they were good.

The sun, just peeking over the horizon, streamed into Adam's room. Adam remembered that plants need light to help them grow.

Sunlight danced off his mirror onto the walls. It shone on his face and made him feel warm. And he saw that the sun was good.

Adam uncovered his bird cage. His parakeet hopped from perch to perch, waiting to be fed. Adam gave her some seeds, and she ate and pecked and gave Adam a loud, squawking whistle of thanks.

"You're welcome," said Adam, as he bent over to feed his fish. His pets were true friends to him, and he knew that they were good.

But Adam was still lonely. He picked up
the cat and padded down the hall to his
parents' bedroom.

"Good morning, honey," said Adam's mother.
"How are things going?" asked his father.

"Everything is perfect." Adam smiled as he
jumped into the bed.

And then, nestled between his mother and father, Adam rested.